Isaiah 26:3-4
"PERFECT PEACE III"

Isaiah 26:3-4

"PERFECT PEACE III"

Silver and Gold

Vanessa Buckhalter

authorHOUSE®

AuthorHouse™
1663 Liberty Drive
Bloomington, IN 47403
www.authorhouse.com
Phone: 1-800-839-8640

Published by AuthorHouse   10/24/2012

ISBN: 978-1-4772-8236-6 (sc)
ISBN: 978-1-4772-8235-9 (e)

A GIFT

*P*resented to

_____

*F*rom

_____

*D*ate

_____

Be Blessed!!!

CONTENTS

THEME

The universal message of this book is Isaiah 26:3-4, "Perfect Peace." This is the distinct and unifying composition of this book with the subtitle Silver and Gold.

Thou wilt keep him in perfect peace, whose mind is stayed on thee: because he trusteth in thee. Trust ye in the LORD for ever: for in the LORD JEHOVAH is everlasting strength. Isaiah 26:3-4 KJV

You will keep in perfect peace those whose minds are steadfast, because they trust in you. Trust in the LORD forever, for the LORD, the LORD himself, is the Rock eternal. Isaiah 26:3-4 NIV

You will keep in perfect peace all who trust in you, all whose thoughts are fixed on you! Trust in the Lord always, for the Lord God is the eternal Rock. Isaiah 26:3-4 NLT

Remember, from Isaiah 26:3-4, "Perfect Peace" ~ The Last Single Digit that Bible translations fall into 3 categories? They are

Formal Equivalence, Functional Equivalence, and Paraphrase.

Formal Equivalence refers to, translating by finding reasonably words and phrases that have equal value, significance or meaning while following the source language as closely as possible. This style is often referred to as "Literal Translation" or "Word-for-Word Translation." Some of the Formal Equivalence translations in English are KJV, ASV, ERV, NASB, ESV, and AMP.

Functional Equivalence is sometimes called "Dynamic Equivalence" or "Thought—for—Thought Translation." It is a translation process in which the translator(s) attempts to reflect and focus on the thought of the writer in the source language rather than the word-for-word translation. The NIV, HCSB, and CEV are some of the popular Functional Equivalence translations.

The Extensive use of Dynamic Equivalence is called a paraphrase, or thought—for-thought translation. It goes even further than dynamic equivalence when translating the source. It conveys some key concepts while not retaining even a dynamic equivalence with the text. Two popular versions of this type are NLT, and MSG.

PRAYER

Father, In the Name of Jesus,
I pray that this book will help your people,
Open their mind, heart, soul, and spirit to You
Daily.

Father God bless those that help make
Your Work and Word able to go forth in a sin—sick
world.

Father, You make it clear that You will reward those
that bless your servant.
It could be by prayer, words of encourage, buying
a book, e-mailing others about the book, to even
given that person a cup of water.

**And *whosoever* shall give to drink unto one
of these little ones a cup of cold water only in
the name of a disciple, verily I say unto you, he
shall in no wise lose his reward.**
Matthew 10:42 KJV

Vanessa Buckhalter

**And if you give even a cup of cold water to one
of the least of my followers,
You will surely be rewarded.**
Matthew 10:42 NLT

Father, I give you all the Glory and Honor because
You are so Worthy.

Amen

AUTHOR'S NOTES

Author notes normally provide a way to add extra information to one's book that may be awkward and inappropriate to include in the text of the book itself. It provides supplemental contextual details on the aspects of the book that are not discussed directly. It can help readers understand the book content and the background details of the book better. The times and dates of researching, reading, and gathering this information are not included; only when I typed on it.

Saturday, 18 February 2012; 2130 watching "The Bodyguard" on Lifetime in memory of Whitney Houston.

Sunday, 19 February 2012; 0416

Tuesday, 21 February 2012; 0200

Saturday, 25 February 2012; 0746

Sunday, 26 February 2012; 1915

Monday, 27 February 2012; 0228

Vanessa Buckhalter

Tuesday, 29 February 2012; 0639

Thursday, 01 March 2012; 1804

Friday, 02 March 2012; 0734

Saturday, 17 March 2012; 0749

Monday, 26 March 2012; 1117

Tuesday, 27 March 2012; 1915

Wednesday, 4 April 2012; 1710

Thursday, 5 April 2012; 0030

Monday, 9 April 2012; 0544, just returned from
Killeen, TX, around midnight

Tuesday, 10 April 2012; 0345

Monday, 16 April 2012; 0742

Saturday, 28 April 2012; 1412

Sunday, 29 April 2012; 1406

Wednesday, 2 May 2012; 2013

Saturday, 5 May 2012; 1412

Wednesday, 30 May 2012; 0756, Thank God! For A New Computer (Samsung with all the trimmings; I'm all smiles) Glory Be To God!!!

Friday, 1 June 2012; around 0745 met an interesting man this morning at the Tennessee DVM. Mr. Larry R. invited me to the Salvation Army's Church Services. He overheard me praying with and for Ms. S. Shields about an issue about her job, on the telephone. He stated, he needs some prayer, and it would be nice to have a Christian friend. That's enough for now . . . smile . . .

Wednesday, 6 June 2012; 0623

Thursday, 7 June 2012; 0559

Sunday, 10 June 2012; 0450

Tuesday, 12 June 2012; 0840

Friday, 15 June 2012; 1422

Saturday, 16 June 2012; 0616

Sunday, 17 June 2012; 0616

Tuesday, 19 June 2012; 1900

Wednesday, 20 June 2012; 1000

Vanessa Buckhalter

Friday, 22 June 2012; 0602

Tuesday, 26 June 2012; 1740

Thursday, 28 June 2012; 1730

Friday, 29 June 2012; 0900

Saturday, 30 June 2012; 1256

Monday, 02 July 2012; 1300

Tuesday, 03 July 2012; 0001

Saturday, 07 July 2012; 1300

Sunday, 08 July 2012; 0719

Tuesday, 10 July 2012; 0923

Wednesday, 11 July 2012; 0856

Friday, 13 July 2012; 0521

Thursday, 19 July 2012; 1442 ~ Mom's birthday

Saturday, 21 July 2012; 1300

Sunday, 22 July 2012; 1344

Tuesday, 24 July 2012; 1223 ~ just picked youngest son up from court. God is good, even when we are not good!!!

Friday, 5 October 2012; 1700 ~ making a few changes for AuthorHouse; then going to e-mail it by 1730 today.

PREFACE

Isaiah 26:3-4, "Perfect Peace" ~ <u>Silver and Gold</u>

This book is the 3rd book of a series of Isaiah 26:3-4, "Perfect Peace" collection; but my 4th book. Glory Be To God! It started from how I drew near to the Lord in my workplace by keeping my mind on Him. I related numbers, you see throughout the day, everywhere on almost everything on Him, His word, biblical events and facts.

This book, <u>Silver and Gold</u>, focus on Acts, chapter 3; verses 1-10. The words in this passage of scriptures that are in bold print will forever relate to you in a more meaningful and spiritual matter. My desire is for you to discover the power of the Holy Spirit by numbers, words, places, people, and things. Remember, the LORD Jesus promised us tribulation, while we were in this world.

These things, I have spoken unto you, that in me ye might have peace.
In the world ye shall have tribulation:

But be of good cheer; I have overcome the world.
John 16:33 KJV

However, we have been promised His peace while we endure these short trials, tribulations, troubles, and tests. Perfect Peace is given only to those whose mind and heart reclines upon the LORD. God's peace is increased in us according to the knowledge the LORD gives to us from His Word.

Grace and peace be multiplied unto you through the knowledge of God, and of Jesus our LORD.
2 Peter 1:2 KJV

It is our hope that the biblical event in Acts 3 will forever be etched in your mind when you see the number 3. You will have an in-depth understanding about the phrase "Hour of Prayer." Whenever you met, someone name Peter or John; you will think about our forefathers' Peter and John along with their contributions to Christianity. When you approach a gate, you think about the miracle that happened at a gate called Beautiful. When you extended your right hand to a person, you know what the Biblical meaning of this act is. When you see the words alms, temple, silver and gold; you will recall this biblical event, more precisely. Hopefully, "The Book of Acts" from this day forward will always bring a smile to your heart, when the Pastor asks you to turn to it. Last but not least, a remarkable truth about "Jesus Christ of Nazareth."

THANKS

First, I'd like to say, as a disciple of the Lord, we can rest assure that when we are seeking His plan and purpose, we will be successful, because true success lies in doing God's will; not in fame and fortune.

Remember, we may not know until we get to heaven just how much a song you have sung, kind words you spoke, or a book you suggested reading, at the right moment have encourage a person to keep on going when a few minutes before they were tempted to give up on life, and maybe their walk with the Lord.

Thanks for your support, and may the Lord bless you; Real Good.

ACKNOWLEDGEMENT

I would like to express my gratitude to all those who have presented me with words of encouragements, especially those who I have never met. I still read your email. Thanks and May God Bless You, Greatly!

Know this my sister. The work is all Divine. One trial + One testimony = One triumph!!!!!!! by Charles L. (10/07)

I would love to read your books. What are the titles of your books and where can I buy them from? by Arnita F. (10/07)

Hello Vanessa, My name is Lee, I work at Baptist Hospital. The other day I found your book marker at work while on my rounds. I picked it up out of curiosity and started to read it. I noticed that you had gone through some pretty hard stuff at your work place. It got my attention was very interesting to me because I have gone through some similar things here at my job. First I will let you know . . . by Lee J. (09/07)

Vanessa Buckhalter

Dr. Vanessa! Dr. Luther here. The text looks promising . . . . I want to encourage you in further pursuits as well . . . . Congratulations on the 'birthing' of this baby. May there be many more children to come for you! Keep the faith. by Luther I. (10/07)

I am sure God has his hand is this. God bless you and nice to meet you. by Tony L. (02/08)

INTRODUCTION

For Those Who Want To Be Kept In "Perfect Peace"

This book was prepared and written to open your mind to a "Perfect Peace" that comes only from God. I'm striving to raise you into a "Unique and Profound" awareness of God's presence around you at all time.

According to some people, it is impossible to keep your mind on the LORD, your God. While most Christians will agree that if you keep your mind stayed on the LORD, he will keep you in "Perfect Peace." This is why so many people enjoy going to church on Sundays and attending midweek services for peace and joy that they receive, but for only for a short time.

Think about that for just a moment, and realize that you can experience the presence and peace of the LORD your God throughout the day and every day. His unspeakable joy, his strength, his "Perfect Peace" in the midst of the storm whether it's at work, home, college, school, etc. You can also experience this peace, even when your day is going well.

This book that you hold in your hands was placed in my spirit by our Father, which art in heaven, to help me when he allowed Satan to test me at my workplace until he finished molding me into a MAP; (Minister/Ambassador/Pastor).

Throughout these pages, I will be focussing on the biblical events and facts about this passage of scriptures, Acts 3:1-10. I will show you how to keep your mind on the LORD by sharing this event in a unique manner. However, much more can be said on this passage of scriptures, so these examples serve merely as an introduction and are not exhaustive by any means.

In the other books to follow, I will concentrate on another number, or set of numbers, or a passage of scriptures. I know you will be enlighten and enjoy the peace it will bring in Jesus' Name.

Watch, what happens around you when you keep your mind on Him, and at the same time you will become familiar with our forefathers and events that occurred.

DEDICATION

I would like to dedicate <u>Silver and Gold</u> to those who are seeking peace, "Perfect Peace" in a Unique and Profound way, in Jesus' name. Amen.

CHAPTER 1

The Event

First may I ask you, what's an "event?" You know there are many types of events. You may have a main event; attend a sport or social event. Hear about the current events, and read about the latest events. I'm sure you can recall other events. Most definitions will say in some shape or fashion an event is happening or occurrences. We hear and read about events every day that are either good, bad, important, beneficial, happy, funny, sad, interesting, exciting, unusual, the true and not true. Writing events are and can be written in several styles. The same, identical event can be written in a general, technical, business, creative, formality, precision, objectivity, explicative or either a casual style.

Today, in this first chapter you are going to read about an event, a Biblical Event. This event happened over 2,000 years ago concerning a lame man. Remember, the Bible along with its Biblical Events is translated into many versions but only three translation writing styles. What are they? The detailed answer is in the 2nd book of the series Isaiah 26:3-4, "Perfect Peace:" <u>The Last Single Digit</u> in chapter 1. In brief, they are "Word for Word Translation", "Thought for Thought" and "Paraphrase Translation."

Now **Peter and John** went up together into the temple at **the hour of prayer**, being the ninth hour. And a certain man lame from his mother's womb was carried, whom they laid daily at the gate of the temple which is called **Beautiful**, to ask alms of them that entered into the temple; who seeing Peter and John about to go into the temple asked alms. And Peter, fastening his eyes upon him with John, said, Look on us. And he gave heed unto them, expecting to receive something of them.

Then Peter said, **Silver and gold** have I none; but such as I have give I thee: In the name of **Jesus Christ of Nazareth** rise up and walk. And he took him by the **right hand**, and lifted him up: and immediately his feet and ankle bones received strength. And he leaping up stood, and walked, and entered with them into the temple, walking, and leaping, and praising God. And all the people saw him walking and praising God: And they knew that it was he which sat for **alms** at the Beautiful gate of the temple: and they were filled with wonder and amazement at that which had happened unto him. Acts 3:1-10 KJV

This passage of scripture is considered the "Word for Word Translation." It is also known as the Formal Equivalence. In this translation, the words are mostly matching between languages. However, a translation into an unrelated language is not and cannot be strictly literal.

The next style, this biblical event is written in is a "Thought for Thought Translation" of the Bible. It is also called Functional Equivalence and Dynamic Equivalence. It attempts to convey an understanding of the thought behind the original text which is conveyed in the rendering of the verses. This is how the same biblical event reads in that style translation.

One day **Peter and John** were going up to the temple at **the time of prayer**—at three in the afternoon. Now a man who was lame from birth was being carried to the temple gate called **Beautiful,** where he was put every day to beg from those going in to the temple courts. When he saw Peter and John about to enter, he asked for money. Peter looked straight at him, as did John. Then Peter said, "Look at us!" So the man gave them his attention, expecting to get something from them.

Then Peter said, "**Silver and gold** I do not have, but what I do have I give you. In the name of **Jesus Christ of Nazareth**, walk." Taking him by his **right hand**, he helped him up, and instantly the man's feet and ankles became strong. He jumped to his feet and began to walk. Then he went with them into the temple courts, walking and jumping, and praising God. When all the people saw him walking and praising God, they recognized him as the same man who used to sit begging at the temple gate called Beautiful, and they were filled with wonder and amazement at what happened to him. Acts 3:1-10 NIV

Now, let's slowly read the "Paraphrase Translation. **Peter and John** went to the Temple one afternoon to take part in the three o'clock prayer service. As they approached the Temple, a lame man from birth was being carried in. Each day he was put beside the Temple gate, the one called **Beautiful** Gate, so he could beg from the people going into the Temple. When he saw Peter and John about to enter, he asked for some money. Peter and John looked at him intently, and Peter said, "Look at us!" So the man gave them his attention, expecting to get something for them.

Then Peter said, "**Silver and gold** I do not have, but what I do have I give you. In the name of **Jesus Christ of Nazareth**, walk." Talking him by the **right hand**, he helped him up, and instantly the man feet's and ankles became strong. He jumped to his feet and began to walk. Then he went with them into the temple courts, walking and jumping, and praising God. When all the people saw him walking and praising God, they recognized him as the same man who used to sit begging at the temple gate called Beautiful, and they were filled with wonder and amazement at what had happened to him. Acts 3:1-10 NLT

Remember, the "Paraphrase Translation" has been put in modern language, along with the author's own words which can be readily understood by the typical reader.

CHAPTER 2

Acts

The "Book of Acts" contains 28 chapters about how early Christianity developed. It is the 5th book of the New Testament. It records how believers were empowered by the Holy Spirit. It tells about the birth of the church, how it spread, and the development of the Church from Jerusalem to Rome, which consisted of approximately 1450 miles mostly by foot. The "Book of Acts" can be outlined as follows:

1. The beginning of the church in chapters 1-7.

2. The persecution and dispersion of the church in chapters 8-12.

3. Paul's 1st missionary journey in chapters 13-15. It was from 45 to 49 AD, and his companions were Barnabas, John, and Mark. It was approximately a 1400 mile journey in which he visited Cyprus and Asia Minor, (Turkey). He was sent by the church of Antioch, Syria. His journey goes like this:

     a.   Acts 13   Paul travelled to Cyprus by the way of Seleucia, then Antioch in Pisidia.

     b.   Acts 14   Paul travelled to Iconium, Lystra in Lycaonia, Derbe and then back through Lystra, Iconium, and Antioch Pisidia. Paul returns to his home church at Antioch, Syria.

     c.   Acts 15   Paul met with the Council of Jerusalem.

4. Paul's 2nd missionary journey in chapters 15-18. It was from 50 to 52 AD, and his companions were Silas, Timothy, Luke, Priscilla and Aquila. During this time, Paul wrote 1st and 2nd Thessalonians from Corinth. It was approximately a 2,800 mile journey in which he visited Syria, Turkey, and Greece. He was sent by the church of Antioch, Syria. The journey goes like this:

     a.   Acts 15   Paul travelled to Syria and Cililia.

     b.   Acts 16   Paul travelled to Derbe and Lystra in Lycaonia, then Phrygia and Galatia, Mysia to Troas, Samothracis and Neapolis

in that order. Chapter 16
ends with Paul at Philippi
in Macedonia.

c.   Acts 17   Paul travelled to
Amphipolis and Apollonia,
Thessalonica, Berea, and
Athens.

d.   Acts 18   Paul travelled to Corinth,
Cenchrea, Ephesus,
Caesarea, Antioch (Syria),
and Jerusalem.

5.   Paul's 3rd missionary journey is recorded in
chapters 18-20. It was from 53 to 58 AD,
and his companions were Timothy, Luke,
and other disciples. During this time Paul
wrote 1st Corinthians from Ephesus, 2nd
Corinthians from Macedonia, and Romans
from Corinth. It was approximately a 2,700
mile journey in which he visited Turkey,
Greece, Lebanon, Judea, Samaria, and
Galilee. He was also sent by the church of
Antioch, Syria. This journey went like this:

a.   Acts 18   Paul travelled to Galatia
and Phrygia.

b.   Acts 19   Paul travelled to Ephesus,
and Macedonia.

    c.   Acts 20   Paul travelled to Greece (Achaia), Macedonia, Philippi and Troas.
He travelled to Assos, Mitylene, Chios, Samos, Trogyllium, and Miletus.

6. Paul's Arrest Ordeal; Chapters 21-27. During this ordeal, and being under house arrest in Rome, Paul wrote four epistles, which are Ephesians, Philippians, Colossians and Philemon. They are also known as the "Prison Epistles."

    a.   Acts 21/22   Paul speaks to the crowd of people.

    b.   Acts 23   Paul speaks before the Sanhedrin.

    c.   Acts 24   Paul speaks before Felix, the Roman procurator, the governor of Judea.

    d.   Acts 25   Paul speaks before Festus, the successor of Felix.

    e.   Acts 26   Paul speaks before King Agrippa.

7. Paul's Voyage to Rome is in chapters 27-28.

The "Book of Acts" centers around the life of two apostles, Peter and Paul. The following person are also mentioned in this book, John, James, Stephen, Barnabas, Timothy, Lydia, Silas, Apollo, Mark, Priscilla and Aquila. Acts 1—12 is about the person and ministry of the Apostle Peter, a Jewish believer. Acts 12—28 is about the person and ministry of Apostle Paul, a gentile believer. Luke, a gentile, a Greek physician, wrote the "Book of Acts" before Jerusalem was destroyed by the Romans in 70 A.D. Luke was also a travelling companion of Paul.

The "Book of Acts" has traditionally been called the "Acts of the Apostles" because it is considered a chronicle of the Apostle's ministry after Christ's death, burial, and resurrection. The "Book of Acts" has also been called the "Acts of the Holy Spirit." The word "Holy Spirit" runs dominant in the "Book of in Acts." It is mentioned 41 times in only 28 chapters, KJV. This title gives the "Holy Spirit" the glory of the "Acts of the Apostles" which includes their preaching, teaching, healing, miracles, raising the dead, signs and wonders that occurred throughout the book of Acts. Let's take a quick look at them:

Acts 2:2-4   All the apostles spoke in others tongues as the Spirit gave them utterance.

Acts 3:1-8	Peter & John heals a lame man.
Acts 4:23-31	The room was shaken & people were filled with the Holy Spirit after the apostles' release from prison and prayed.
Acts 5:1-10	Peter sentenced Ananias & Sapphira to be miraculously struck dead.
Acts 5:12—16	Sick people were healed by Peter's shadow passing over them.
Acts 5:17-19	All the Apostles were freed from prisons by an angel.
Acts 8:14-17	Peter & John bestowed miraculous powers to other by laying their hands on them.
Acts 9:1-9	Paul received visions from the Lord.
Acts 9:15-15	The Lord spoke to Ananias.
Acts 9:32-35	Bedridden and paralyzed man was healed by Peter.

Acts 9:36-43   Peter raised Dorcas from the dead.

Acts 10:44-46   Peter preached to the first Gentile converts, who began speaking in tongues.

Acts 12:5-12   Peter was freed by an angel in prison.

Acts 13:8-12   Paul condemned and struck Elymas blind.

Acts 14:8-10   Paul heals a crippled man in Lystra.

Acts 16:9-10   Paul received visions from God to help a man in Macedonia.

Acts 16:16-18   Paul casts out an evil spirit in a female slave, fortune-teller.

Acts 16:25-26   An earthquake opened all the doors and released all the chains in a prison, where Paul and Silas were housed.

Acts 18:9-10   Paul received visions from the Lord.

Acts 19:6   Paul laid hands on people, imparting the Holy Spirit, by which they spoke in tongues and prophesied.

Acts 19:11-12 Handkerchiefs and aprons that Paul touched could be used to heal people and cast out evil spirits.

Acts 19:13-17 A demon publicly recognizes Jesus and Paul, when seven sons of Sceva, unsanctioned people attempt to cast out the demon.

Acts 20:7-12 Paul raised Eutychus from the dead, after he fell out of a third story window.

Acts 22:17-21 Paul received visions from the Lord in a trace.

Acts 27:23-25 Paul received a message and prophecy from an angel.

Acts 28:3-6 Paul was bit by a deadly viper, and didn't die.

Acts 28:7-10 Paul heals Publius' father and many others on the island.

The "Acts of the Apostles" shares the same author as the "Gospel of Luke." This is suggested by the dedication to "Theophilus" which is at the beginning of both books. Theophilus means "Love of God" or "Friend of God."

The former treatise have I made,
O Theophilus,
of all that Jesus began both to do and teach.
Acts 1:1 KJV

Forasmuch as many have taken in hand to set
forth in order
a declaration of those things which are most
surely believed among us,
Even as they delivered them unto us, which
from the beginning were
eyewitnesses, and ministers of the world;

It seems good to me also, having had perfect
understanding of all things
from the very first, to write unto thee in order,
most excellent Theophilus.
Luke 1:1-3 KJV

The "Book of Acts" has been called the 5th Gospel. It is considered a continuation of the gospel Luke. The "Book of Acts" is unique in other ways. In Matthew's gospel, the last chapter speaks of Jesus' resurrection; and that's recorded in Acts 1. In Mark's gospel, Jesus' ascension is recorded in the last chapter; and that's recorded in Acts 1. In Luke's gospel, the promise of the Holy Spirit is recorded in the last chapter; and that's in Acts 1. In John's gospel, the promise of the 2nd coming of Jesus Christ is mention in the last chapter; and that's recorded in Acts 1. The "Great Missionary Commission" given in the four gospels is confirmed in the "Book of Acts," also.

The "Book of Acts" covers about 30 years after the ascension of Jesus Christ into heaven. The theme verse in Acts is Acts 1:8 which is Jesus' commission to the Apostles.

But ye shall receive power, after the Holy Ghost is come upon you:
and ye shall witnesses unto me both in Jerusalem,
and all Judea, and in Samaria,
and unto the uttermost part of the earth.
Acts 1:8 KJV

Based on the theme verse the "Book of Acts" can be divided as follows:

1. Chapters 1-7; The Lord Jesus Christ at work by the Holy Spirit through the Apostles in Jerusalem; 30 A.D.

2. Chapters 8-12; The Lord Jesus Christ at work by the Holy Spirit through the Apostles in Judea and Samaria; 30-43 A.D.

3. Chapters 13-28; The Lord Jesus Christ at work by the Holy Spirit through the Apostles to the uttermost parts of the earth, to Rome, the capital of the Gentiles; 43—62 A.D.

Throughout the "Book of Acts," the Holy Spirit is revealed working through the Apostles. The "Book of Acts" has no proper ending. Most every New Testament books ends with the word, "Amen." The Book of Acts end with Paul at his own rented house welcoming all that came to visit. He was teaching and proclaiming the kingdom of God to all who visit him.

**And Paul dwelt two whole years in his own hired house,
and received all that came in unto him,
Preaching the kingdom of God,
and teaching those things which concern Lord Jesus Christ,
with all confidence, no man forbidding him.**
Acts 28:30-31 KJV

CHAPTER 3

Peter and John

Peter and John are two of the first twelve originally disciples of Jesus Christ. Peter is considered the "Apostle of Faith," and John is called the "Apostle of Love. Now please, take a moment, and listed the other ten. Remember, they are OUR forefathers, whom made it possible for you and me to know about Jesus Christ, the Savior of the world! LORD, I thank You! Glory Be To God!

1. _____

2. _____

3. _____

4. _____

5. _____

6. _____

7. _____

8. _____

9. _____

10. _____

In case, you need a little help look in the back of the book. Smile ☺

Now let me think . . .

In the bible, Peter is also known as Simon. Peter's originally name was Simon Barjona. Jesus changed his name to Peter, which means stone/rock in Greek. Peter was also called by the name "Cephas" which also means stone/rock; but in Aramaic.

And he (Andrew) **brought him** (Simon) **to Jesus.
And when Jesus beheld him, he said,
Thou art Simon the son of Jona: thous shalt be called Cephas,
which is by interpretation, A stone.**
John 1:42 KJV

Peter and John brothers', Andrew and James were disciples of Jesus, also. They were all fishermen when Jesus called them to follow Him.

The Apostle Peter was born in Bethsaida near the lake of Galilee. His brother Andrew is the one who introduced him to Jesus. They were disciples of John the Baptist, at first. These two brothers were named "Sons of Thunder" by Jesus, Mark 3.

James son of Zebedee and his brother John

**(to them he gave the name Boanerges, which
means "sons of thunder").**
John 3:17 NIV

Peter is well-known for stating he would die
before denying Christ, to which our Lord replied,
**"I tell you Peter, before the cock crow, thou
shalt deny me thrice,"** recorded in 26th chapter
of Matthew, 14th chapter of Mark, 22nd chapter of
Luke, and 13th chapter of John. Peter in Matthew
14, attempts to walk on water as Jesus, and was
the first to declare publicly that Jesus was the
Messiah, Matthew 16.

**And he said, Come.
And when Peter was come down out of the
ship,
he walked on the water, to go to Jesus.**
Matthew 14:29 KJV

**And Simon Peter answered and said,
Thou art the Christ, the Son of the living God.**
Matthew 16:16 KJV

Peter was also rebuked by Jesus in Matthew
16, and in John 18 he cut off Malchus' ear,
a servant of the high priest Caiaphas, who
participated in Jesus' arrested. Peter's father was
named Jona. Peter had an unnamed wife, whose
mother Jesus healed from a terrible fever, Matthew
8:14.

After Jesus' death, burial, resurrection, and ascension, Peter and John played a prominent part in the development of the early Church. Later Peter had a vision in Acts 10 from the Holy Spirit which led him to accept the Gentile believers.

Peter died at Rome during Nero's persecution of Christians in 64 A.D. He was crucified but begged to be crucified upside down instead because he felt he wasn't worthy to be crucified in the manner as his Savior.

Since Peter death, the church in Rome claimed special prestige from his life and death in their city. He is considered the first Bishop of Rome. The Vatican Basilica of St. Peter's is said to be built above the site of his martyrdom. Peter was given the most prominence by the Church in the time of Pope Leo the Great. Since then, all Popes claim a spiritual descendant from Peter.

John is mentioned in all of the Gospels, and three other books of the bible; Acts, Galatians, and Revelation. He wrote five books of the Bible; "The Gospel of John," 1st John, 2nd John, 3rd John, and Revelation." He was the last Apostle to die. John out lived Peter about 30 years. Peter is also mentioned in all the Gospels, and the book of Acts, Galatians, 1st & 2nd Peter. Peter only wrote two books of the Bible.

John wrote what is perhaps the most familiar and quoted scripture in the New Testament.

For God so loved the world,
that He gave His only begotten Son,
that whosoever believeth in Him should not
perish,
but have everlasting life.
John 3:16 KJV

John wrote a lot about love and the
commandments. John was also one especially
loved by Jesus, according to John 21:20.

Peter turned and saw that the disciple whom
Jesus loved was following them.
John 21:20 NIV
John was the only apostle to use the terms
antichrist in 1st John 4:3 and 2nd John 1:7.

And every spirit that confesseth not that Jesus
Christ
is come in the flesh is not of God:
and this is the spirit of the antichrist,
whereof ye have heard that it should come;
and even now already is in the world.
1st John 4:3 KJV

For many deceivers are entered into the world,
who confess not that Jesus Christ is come in
the flesh.
This is a deceiver and an antichrsit.
2nd John 1:7

Throughout the New Testament, Peter and John are oftentimes together as companions to each other, doing the work of the Lord. John and Peter had a prominent position in the apostolic body. Peter, James, and John were the only witnesses of the raising of Jairus's daughter in Mark 5:37. They witnessed the Transfiguration of Jesus in Matthew 17:1; and the agony of Jesus in Gethsemane recorded in Matthew 26.

Only Peter and John were sent into the city, to make the preparation for the Last Supper in Luke 22:8. At the supper, John place was next to Jesus on whose bosom he leaned on according to John 13:23-25.

John was the other disciple, who with Peter followed Jesus after the arrest into the palace of the high priest in John 18:15. John alone stood faithfully at the cross with the mother of Jesus, his mother's sister, Mary the wife of Clopas, and Mary Magdalene. John took Jesus' mother into his care after his death, John 19:25-27.

After His resurrection, John with Peter was the first of the disciples to hasten to the grave, and believed that Jesus had risen according to John 20:2-10. Later Jesus appeared at the sea of Tiberias, John was also the first of the seven disciples present who recognized his LORD standing on the shore in John 21:7.

**Therefore that disciple whom Jesus loved said
unto Peter,
It is the Lord.
Now when Simon Peter heard that it was the
Lord,
he girt his fisher's coat unto him, (for he was
naked,) and did cast himself into the sea.**
John 21:7 KJV

After Jesus' Ascension and the Descent of
the Holy Spirit, John together with Peter, played a
prominent part in the founding and leadership of
the Church. John is in the company of Peter at the
healing of the lame man at the Temple, Acts 3:1.
John is with Peter when they are thrown in prison,
Acts 4:3. Again, we find him with the Apostles
visiting the newly converted in Samaria according
to Acts 8:14.

Jesus even gave both of them a mutual
assignment, recorded in Luke22.

**Jesus sent Peter and John ahead and said, "
Go and prepare the Passover meal,
so we can eat it together.**
Luke 22:8 NLT

And it was both Peter and John that saw Jesus
transfigured, according to Luke 9.

**And it came to pass about eight days after
these sayings,**

**He took Peter and John and James and went
up into a mountain to pray.
And as He prayed, the fashion of His
countenance was altered,
and His raiment was white and glistering.**
Luke 9:28-29 NLT

Jesus frequently trained the two of them
together.

**And He suffered no man to follow Him,
save Peter, and James, and John the brother of
James.**
Mark 5:37 KJV

Matthew 26:36-37 states,

**Then cometh Jesus with them unto a place
called Gethsemane,
and saith unto the disciples,
Sit ye here, while I go and pray yonder.
And He took with Him Peter and the two sons
of Zebedee,
and began to be sorrowful and very heavy.**
Matthew 26:36-37 KJV

James and John were the sons of Zebedee,
according to Matthew 4:21. John was the younger
brother of James. They were the cousins of Jesus.
Their mother named was Salome, Mary's younger
sister.

Apostle John found many churches in Asia Minor, which is now modern-day Turkey. Asia Minor consists of Ephesus, Smyrna, Pergamum, Thyatira, Sardis, Philadelphia, and Laodicea. The seven churches that Revelation, chapters 3 and 4 speak of.

Later, John was brought to Rome, by the orders of Emperor Domitian. He was cast into a cauldron of boiling oil but came forth unhurt and was banished to the island of Patmos for a year. There, he wrote the book of Revelation, the last book of the New Testament.

He lived to an extreme old age, surviving all his fellow apostles. The "beloved disciple" died at Ephesus about 100 A.D. A church was erected over his tomb. It was later converted into a Mohammedan Mosque which is a place for religious worship.

I just can't resist this question for some reason! I feel in my soul this will bless someone. Encourage you to spread the gospel more, praise and worship God better.

How did the other disciples of Jesus die for **US**, so that, the Gospel could be preached in all the nations? (Answer in back of the book) ☺

CHAPTER 4

Hour of Prayer

Now Peter and John went up together into the temple at **the hour of prayer**, being the ninth hour, Acts 3:1. These four words, "The Hour of Prayer," in the above Bible verse are unique and profound all by themselves. Oftentimes, we "read over" without truly understanding the depth of it. This chapter will expound on "The Hour of Prayer."

The three daily historic times of prayer in Biblical hours are specifically the third hour, sixth hour, and the ninth hour of the day. These times were significant, respected and observed by the Old Testament Saints, the New Testament Church, and by the Lord Jesus Christ and the disciples.

Evening, and morning, and at noon will I pray, and cry aloud:
and he shall hear my voice.
Psalm 55:17 KJV

Evening: Psalm 117 was read; only two verses.

Morning: The Lord's Prayer, Matthew 6:9-13 was read.

Noon: The Lord is my Shepherd, 23rd Psalm was read.

(These three prayers are in the back of book for your convenience)

The first hour of prayer is at 9am, called the 3rd hour. This is when the Temple gates are opened. The second hour of prayer is noon, called the 6th hour. It is also known as the "Hour of Confession." The third hour of prayer was at 3pm, called the 9th hour. The biblical days began at sundown, or about 6pm.

The Early Christians continued the Jewish practice of reciting prayers at certain hours of the day or night. In the book of Psalms, you will find expression like "in the morning I offer you my prayer," "At midnight I will rise," "Evening, morning, and at noon I will cry and lament," "Seven times a day I praise you."

Jesus' Apostles knew that prayer was a vital role in the believer's life. They even asked Jesus to teach them to pray.

One day Jesus was praying in a certain place. When He finished, one of his disciples said to him,
"Lord teach us to pray, just as John taught his disciple."

Luke 11:1 NIV

Prayer is an essential element to God and man relationship to God. God said in Isaiah 56:7, "for my house will be called a house of prayer for all nations."

In the Old Testament, the hours of prayer were known as the hours of "Sacrifice" or "Oblation," according to Daniel 9:21. Oblation is the act of offering something, such as worship or thanks, to a God.

Yea, while I was speaking in prayer, even the man Gabriel,
whom I had seen in the vision at the beginning, being caused to fly swiftly,
touched me about the time of the evening oblation.
Daniel 9:21 KJV

The New Testament is filled with accounts of how God has honored these particular hours. It was the third hour on the day of Pentecost, when the 120 disciples were in the upper room praying for the promise of the Father, Acts 2:1-15.

For these are not drunken, as ye suppose, seeing it is but the third hour of the day.
Acts 2:15 KJV

The New Testament Church customarily went to the temple at the hours of prayer. Peter and John went up together into the temple at the hour of prayer, being the ninth hour, Acts 3:1.

On this occasion, a lame man was healed when the Apostle Peter took him by the hand and said, "Silver and gold have I none; but such as I have give I thee: In the name of Jesus Christ of Nazareth rise up and walk." Immediately, this man feet and ankle bones received strength; Acts 3:6-7. They were not at the temple by happenstance entering the temple but decidedly, deliberately and faithful doing so at the hour of prayer.

Now let's look at the biblical event of the Apostle Peter and Cornelius of Caesarea in Acts 10. Cornelius was a soldier in the roman army. Even though, he was a soldier for the roman's army, he was a righteous man who prayed to God always and was exceedingly generous in his almsgiving. He was in prayer about the ninth hour when an angel of the Lord appeared to him in a vision. The angel instructs Cornelius to send men to Joppa, and call for one Simon, whose surname is Peter.

The next day as Cornelius' servants came to Joppa, Peter had a spiritual experience. Peter was on the house rooftop praying about the sixth hour. Suddenly, he fell into a trance and saw a vision of a large linen cloth being let down from heaven full of all kinds of unclean beasts. God proceeded to tell Peter to receive these Gentiles because they had now been cleansed. This prepared Peter for ministry to the Gentiles people, whom he considered unacceptable for the kingdom of God. Peter obedience to God resulted in a great outpouring of the Holy Spirit upon the household of Cornelius and the Gentile nations.

The Seven Historical Hours of Prayer in reference to Psalm119 are listed below.

Seven times a day do I praise thee because of thy righteous judgments.
Psalm 119:164 KJV

6am	—	First Hour	Psalm 5
9am	**—**	**Third Hour**	**The Lord's Prayer**
Noon —		**Sixth Hour**	**23rd Psalm**
3pm	**—**	**Ninth Hour**	**Psalm 117**
6pm	—	Evensong	Psalm 150
9pm	—	Compline	Psalm 4

Midnight Prayers Psalm 119:62; Psalm 134

The observances of the three times a day prayer can serve as a reminder of our Lord's ultimate sacrifice of Himself on our behalf. The three prayers are related to the Crucifixion of Christ. Chirst was crucified for us at the 3rd hour. Then at the 6th hour, darkness came over the land and lasted until the 9th hour. At the 9th hour is when our Lord gave up His spirit. Christ, our Passover, gave up His spirit at the time of the Evening Sacrifice.

And the superscription of His accusation was written over,
The King of the Jews."
"And when the sixth hour was come,
there was darkness over the whole land until the ninth hour.
"And at the ninth hour Jesus cried with a loud voice,
saying, Eloi, Eloi, Lama Sabachthani?
Which is, being interpreted, My God, My God, why hast thou forsaken Me?"
Mark 15:25, 33-34 KJV

In conclusion, prayer is significant at any hour of the day. God has given us prayer as a means of communion with and growing closer, to Him.

CHAPTER 5

Beautiful

Acts 3:2, "And a certain man lame from his mother's womb was carried, whom they laid daily at the gate of the temple which is called **Beautiful**, to ask alms of them that entered the temple."

According to the Bible, the Beautiful Gate was one of the gates belonging to the Temple in Jerusalem prior to its destruction by the Roman army in 70 A.D under the leadership of Titus while Vespasian was the emperor. The destruction of the Temple in Jerusalem was also prophesied by Jesus, Matthew 23:31-39, Matthew 24, Mark 13:1-37, and Luke 21:5-36.

Nevertheless, Beautiful Gate was added by Herod the Great, between the court of the Gentiles and that of Israel. Gate Beautiful mentioned in Acts 3:2 and 10 were also referred to as the "Gate Susan." During the time of the morning and evening sacrifices, this grand entrance was the place of public worshiped.

Attempts by scholars to agree on the identity of the gate have met with little success. The upper inner gate called the Nicanor, and the lower outer gate called the Shushan have been suggested. Scholars are divided as to whether this gate was situated at the entrance to the women's court on the East, or was this the gate that reached 15 steps, dividing that court from the court the men.

Josephus, a Jewish priest, scholar and historian records that the temple has nine gates. They were covered in gold and silver on every side; along with the side posts and lintels. Gate Beautiful was the name given to the gate that was thought to be the gate that opens towards "The Mount of Olives" also known as Mount Olivet where at the foot of the mount lies the Garden of Gethsemane.

Josephus, who calls it the gate of Nicanor, describes it as wonderfully rich and beautiful. The magnitudes of the other gates were equal to one another, but Beautiful was much larger for its height was fifty cubits (75ft.), and its doors were forty cubits (60ft). It was adorned having a much richer and thicker plates of silver and gold compare to others. It was made of Corinthian brass, a metal which gave the gate an impressive appearance. It workmanship was more elaborated than those that were covered with silver and gold.

Corinthian Brass was also known as Corinthian Bronze and Corinthiacum. It was a particularly precious metal alloy in classical antiquity. It was thought to be a blend of copper mixed with gold or silver or both, although it has been contended that it was simply an exceptionally high grade of bronze, or a kind of bronze manufactured in Corinth. It is referred to in various ancient texts, but there are no known examples of Corinthian Bronze existing today.

According to this passage of scriptures, Acts 3:1-10; it was now the hour of prayer, and the people were going to the temple to pray. This gate had both men and women entering here. It's here lay the lame man asking alms of them that entered the temple to perform their religious exercises. They were thought to be more compelled to do acts of charity. These were known to be Jews, of whom only alms were to be asked and taken from. It was common for the poor to be placed at gates where their condition would appeal to the multitudes entering for worship. In bible days, public and local charities were virtually unknown, and the helpless were compelled to beg.

The Old City of Jerusalem consisted of 9 gates. The 9th gate called the Eastern Gate, is blocked up and shut, waiting for the arrival of the Messiah. The Eastern Gate was identified by the Prophet Ezekiel in Ezekiel 44, "the Prince will enter through this gate, and He will eat bread before the Lord."

**Then he brought me back
the way of the gate of the outward sanctuary
which looketh toward the east; and it was shut.
Then said the LORD unto me;**

this gate shall be shut, it shall not be opened,
and no man shall enter in by it;
because the LORD, the God of Israel,
hath entered in by it, therefore it shall be shut.
It is for the prince; the prince,
he shall sit in it to eat bread before the LORD;
he shall enter by the way of the porch of that
gate,
and shall go out by the way of the same.
Ezekiel 44:1—3 KJV

The Judeo-Christian believes that the Messiah will enter through the Eastern Gate. Their faith is based on the continuity between Jewish and Christian tradition, between Isaiah and Jesus. This gate, the Eastern Gate, is shut and no one is allowed to enter the Temple Mount from the east. Another name for this gate is the Golden Gate better known as Gate Beautiful where Peter heals a lame man, recorded in Acts 3.

When Jesus entered Jerusalem on Palm Sunday, he was sitting on an ass, and the colt the foal of an ass, the crowds shouted, "Hosanna to the Son of David!" It's thought that Jesus entered the Temple courtyard through this gate, Matthew 21, Mark 11, and John 12. Jesus then proceeded to drive out all those who were selling and buying there, and he overturned the tables of the money changers, and benches of those selling doves, Matthew 21:12.

The names of the nine gates of the Old City of Jerusalem are:

1. The Dung, the lowest gate located in the south.

2. Next to the Dung Gate is the Tanner Gate.

3. The Zion Gate is on the southwest perimeter which leads from the tomb of King David and the Upper Room on Mount Zion into the Armenian and the Jewish Quarters of the Old City.

4. The gate called Jaffa is located on the western perimeter right above the Hinnom Valley.

5. The New Gate is located on the north-western perimeter of the walled city.

6. The Damascus Gate is the busiest gate on Fridays and Saturdays.

7. Herod's Gate, also called Flowers Gate is located on the north-eastern perimeter.

8. Lion Gate, located on the eastern perimeter of the Old City. It is also called St. Stephen's Gate. Tradition has it that Stephen, the 1st martyr was stoned in the Kidron Valley below.

9. Last but not least, Gate Beautiful also known as the Eastern Gate and Golden Gate.

P.S. It's just done on me! The Nine Gates of Jerusalem could have been included in the book title Isaiah 26:3-4, "Perfect Peace" The Last Single-Digit.

~ ~ ~

If you read, Isaiah 26:3-4, "Perfect Peace" <u>The Last Single-Digit</u>, **YOU** would understand what I'm talking about. Glory Be To God! Smile . . .

CHAPTER 6

Silver and Gold

The silver is mine, and the gold is mine, saith the LORD of hosts.

Haggai 2:8 KJV

According to Acts 3:2—6, a man who was lame from birth was being carried to the temple gate called Beautiful. This was the location he was put every day to beg from those going into the temple courts. It was customary for all those who entered the temple to carry some money with them, for the purposes of giving alms to the poor, lame, and crippled.

When he saw Peter and John about to enter, he asked them for money. Peter looked straight at him, as did John. Then Peter said, "Look at us!" So the man gave them his attention, expecting to get something from them. Then Peter said, "**Silver and gold** have none; but such as I have I give thee: In the name of Jesus Christ of Nazareth rise up and walk, KJV. Now, the NIV reads, "Then Peter said, "**Silver or gold** I do not have, but what I do have I give you. In the name of Jesus Christ of Nazareth, walk." Here's the NLT version, "But Peter said, "I don't have any **silver or gold** to give you. But I'll give you what I have. In the name of Jesus Christ of Nazareth, get up and walk!"

In the New Testament, the Greek words khrysos and khrysion are used as a reference to ornaments, coins, and gold in general. Zahav, charuts, kethem, paz, seghor, and ophir are Hebrew terms that refer to gold. The words drachme and argurion are Greek words that refer to silver coins and pieces. Kesef is the word for silver in Hebrew.

Gold is the first and most frequent mentioned metal in the Bible. Silver is mention in the King James Bible 283 times, but gold is mention 419 times. Silver and gold are mentioned 29 times together in the Bible, but only twice in the New Testament.

Then Peter said,
"Silver and gold have I none; but such as I have I give thee:
In the name of Jesus Christ of Nazareth rise up and walk."
Acts 3:6 KJV

Forasmuch as ye know
that ye were not redeemed with corruptible things,
from your vain conversation received by tradition from your fathers;

**But with the precious blood of Christ,
as a lamb without blemish and without spot:**
1 Peter 1:18—19 KJV

Gold and silver are from God and has been given to man for a useful purpose on earth. The first mention of gold is in Genesis 2, describing the river that parted into four headwaters, which watered the Garden of Eden.

**The name of the first is the Pison:
That is it which compassed the whole land of
Havilah, where there is gold;**
Genesis 2:11 KJV

However, silver is mentioned much later in the book of Genesis describing Abram's wealth, better known as Abraham.

**And Abram was very rich in cattle, in silver, and
in gold.**
Genesis 13:2 KJV

Gold, silver, seed, and flour were all used as money. Gold and silver were used in the workings and furnishings of the Ark of the Covenant which is first mentioned by God in Exodus 25. The vessels in the temple were also of gold.

In the Bible, gold is likened to wisdom, faith, and knowledge. Psalms states that God's laws and commandments are more desirable than gold, Psalm 19:7-10, and Psalm119.

The law of thy mouth is better unto me than thousands of gold and silver.
Psalm 119:72 KJV

Psalms also says that while gold has great and considerable value, it is unable to give life, Psalms 49:6-8. Job says that no amount of gold can buy the wisdom that comes from God, Job 28:12-28. Some of Solomon's sayings about silver and gold are:

Choose a good reputation over great riches; being held in high esteem is better than silver and gold.
Proverbs 22:1 NLT

Choose my instruction rather than silver, and knowledge rather than pure gold.
Proverbs 8:10 NLT

How much better to get wisdom than gold, and good judgement than silver!
Proverbs 16:16 NLT

Fire tests the purity of silver and gold, but the LORD tests the heart.
Proverbs 17:3 NLT

When Israel captured cities, God commanded them not to use the captured gold and silver for themselves excepted for the capture of Jericho. Jericho's gold and silver were turned over to the priest and put into the treasury of the house of the LORD, according to Joshua 6:16—24.

The Apostle Peter said one's faith is greater value than gold, which can withstand fire, but be worn away by other means, 1 Peter 1:7. No amount of silver nor gold can deliver one in the day of God's anger, Zephaniah 1:18.

Neither their silver nor their gold shall be able to deliver them in the day of the LORD's wrath; but the whole land shall be devoured by the fire of his jealousy: for he shall make even a speedy riddance of all them that dwell in the land.
Zephaniah 1:18 KJV

CHAPTER 7

Jesus Christ
of
Nazareth

In the name of "**Jesus Christ of Nazareth**" rise up and walk, Acts 3:6. This chapter will expound on "Jesus Christ of Nazareth." This is the name that Peter spoke to heal the lame man that day sitting at the temple gate asking for alms from those who went into the temple for the hour of prayer.

The phrase "Jesus Christ of Nazareth" is mentioned only twice in the King James Bible, and both times it is spoken by Peter in the book of Acts.

Then Peter said,
Silver and gold have I none; but such as I have give I thee:
In the name of Jesus Christ of Nazareth rise up and walk.
Acts 3:6 KJV

Be it known unto you all, and to all the people of Israel,

**that by the name of Jesus Christ of Nazareth,
whom ye crucified, whom God raised from the
dead,
even by him doth this man stand here before
you whole.**
Acts 4:10 KJV

The phrase "Jesus Christ of Nazareth" is extremely powerful. He is the "Christ" which means the "Anointed One," or the "Messiah." The word "Christ" comes from the Greek translation of the Hebrew word "Messiah." The name "Jesus" is derived from the Hebrew-Aramaic word "Yeshua" which means "Yahweh." Yahweh means "the LORD is salvation" or "God saves." Nazareth is the place where Jesus was raised.

The child born of the Virgin Mary will be called Jesus, "for he will save his people from their sins." This is the message that the angel of the LORD gave Joseph.

**And she shall bring forth a son,
and thou shalt call his name Jesus:
for he shall save his people from their sins.**
Matthew 1:21 KJV

**"Neither is there salvation in any other:
for there is none other name under heaven
given among men,
whereby we must be saved."**
Acts 4:12 KJV

Jesus' life, message, and ministry are recorded in the books of Matthew, Mark, Luke and John. These books are considered the four Gospel of the New Testament. Most Bible scholars agree that Jesus was a Jewish teacher and prophet from Galilee who performed many signs, miracles of healing and deliverance.

The Bible explains clearly that Jesus was conceived of the Holy Spirit, and born of a virgin. The angel Gabriel gave him the name Jesus which expresses both his identity and his mission. He was born in a stable in Bethlehem of Judea around 5BC and grew up in Nazareth in Galilee. Jesus' earthly father, Joseph, was a carpenter by trade.

In Mark 6:3, Jesus is referred to as a carpenter. Jesus' mother name is Mary. His brothers are named James, Joseph, Judas and Simon by his earthy father Joseph, according to Mark 3:31, Mark 6:3, Matthew 12:46, Matthew 13:55, and Luke 8:19. Jesus also had sisters but their names are not mention, according to Matthew 13:55-56 and Mark 6:3.

He was baptized by John the Baptist, Matthew 3:13-17. He called 12 Jewish men to follow him which he trained and prepared them to carry on the ministry, Matthew 10:1-4.

He lived a sinless life, even though; he was tempted and tested by satan, Matthew 4:1-11. He turned water into wine at a wedding, John 2. He healed many sick, blind, crippled, and lame people.

Jesus forgave people of their sins. He multiplied fishes and loaves of bread to feed thousands on more than one occasion.

Jesus delivered the demon possessed people, he walked on water, he calmed the stormy sea, and he raised people from the dead. Jesus Christ proclaimed the "Good News" of the Kingdom of God.

He laid down his life and was crucified in 30AD. Jesus Christ was crucified in Jerusalem by the roman governor Pontius Pilate, for claiming to be the King of the Jews. He descended into hell and took the keys of death and hell. Three days after his death, he resurrected, appeared to his disciples and then ascended into heaven.

Jesus Christ paid for the sins of the world. He restored man's fellowship with God. His death provided the atoning sacrifice for the sins of the world. Adam's sin separated us from God, but we were reconciled back to God through Jesus Christ's sacrifice. The Bible states, he will claim us as his Bride, the church. Jesus will return later at his Second Coming to judge the world and establish his eternal kingdom. These are just a few of his outstanding accomplishments.

Jesus Christ's accomplishments are too numerous to list, according to His disciple John.

This is the disciple which testifieth of these things,
and wrote these things: and we know that his testimony is true.
And there are also many other things which Jesus did,
the which, if they should be written every one,
I suppose that even the world itself could not contain the books
that should be written.
Amen.
John 21:24—25 KJV

The date of Jesus' birth to Mary is celebrated each December 25th as Christmas Day. The date of the crucifixion is now marked as Good Friday, and the resurrection celebrated as Easter.

Jesus most famous statement is recorded in John 14.

Jesus answered,
"I am the way and the truth and the life.
No one comes to the Father except through me.
John 14:6 NIV

CHAPTER 8

Right Hand

The phrase "right hand" in the King James Version of the bible is uniquely intriguing. Most people who read this passage, "And he (Peter) took him by the **right hand** (the lame man), and lifted him up: and immediately his feet and ankle bones received strength," just thinks it happen to be the hand Peter extended to the lame man. In reality, it actually refers to several things depending upon the context in which it is used in the Bible. This chapter wants you to look at the "**right hand**" in a unique and profound way from this day forward.

The human hands have a distinctive identity. They are called the right hand and the left hand. The hand consists of 54 bones separated in three distinct regions, the wrist, the palm and the finger digits. Each hand has five finger digits, the number for grace. They are called thumb, which is oftentimes not considered a finger. Next is the pointer finger, sometimes called index finger. The 3rd finger is called the middle finger, which is our longer finger. The ring finger is our 4th finger. The pinky finger or sometimes the little finger is our 5th finger. The four fingers by themselves are weak, but the thumb provides strength and support to the hand, which is an illustration of the LORD's grace. There are 15 finger joints in each hand, 14 for the fingers and 1 for the wrist. Regardless of the millions of people in the world, no two hands have the same set of fingerprints. The bible is filled with scriptures about the hand.

However, the phrase "right hand" is used in over a 160 different verses in the King James Bible; but the "left hand" only 27 times. These scriptures refer to the right hand as:

1. Blessing   Genesis 48:17-20

2. Power   Exodus 15:1-6

3. Service   1 Chronicles 6:33-48

4. Pleasures   Psalm 16:11

5. Salvation   Psalm 17:6-9

6. Sustainment   Psalm 18:30-36

7. Victory   Psalm 44:1-3

8. Righteousness   Psalm 48:10

9. The Messiah   Psalm 110:1

10. Guidance   Psalm 139:1-10

11. Worship   Psalm 118:14-17

12. Wisdom   Proverbs 3:13-18

13. Confidence   Isaiah 41:11-13

14. Creator   Isaiah 48:12-13

The right hand is considered a place of distinction. It represents approval, power, and authority according to Genesis 48:10-22. The right hand placement played a crucial role in Jacob's final blessing to his grandsons. In fact, Joseph, Jacob's son had placed his sons Ephraim at the left side of his father Jacob and placed Manasseh on the right side, expecting his father to place his right hand on Manasseh, the firstborn and his left hand on Ephraim, and then bless them. Instead, Jacob crosses his hands, placing his right hand on Ephraim and his left on Manasseh, despite Joseph concerns. Jacob explains his actions by stating that Ephraim, the youngest, will be greater than Manasseh. It is the Jewish customs to place the right hand on the oldest son, when you bless him.

But Joseph was upset when he saw that his father placed his right hand on Ephraim's head.
So Joseph lifted it to move it from Ephraim's head to Manasseh's head.
"No, my father," he said. "This one is the firstborn.

Put your right hand on his head." But his father refused.
I know my son; I know," he replied.
"Manasseh will also become a great people, but his younger brother will become even greater.
And his descendants will become a multitude of nations."
Genesis 48:17-18 NLT

In the Old Testament, the right hand of the High Priest was anointed with the blood of the sacrifice of consecration. Our God let us know, it's with his right hand, He will uphold us in battle.

Fear thou not; for I am with thee: be not dismayed; for I am thy God:
I will strengthen thee; yea, I will help thee; yea, I will uphold thee with the right hand of my righteousness.
Isaiah 41:10 KJV

The right hand in combat is noteworthy as it is of greater value when holding a weapon. It would be the hand targeted by the enemy, since it would be the most vulnerable with the shield being held in the left hand. When given the right hand after a battle symbolizes submission to the victor.

The right hand is a place of wisdom, as opposed to foolishness, according to Ecclesiastes 10.

A wise man's heart is at his right hand; but fool's heart at his left.
Ecclesiastes 10:2 KJV

When the right hand is given it is a signed of approval and agreement, according to Galatians 2.

And when James, Cephas, and John, who seemed to be pillars, perceived the grace that was given unto me, they gave to me and Barnabas the right hands of fellowship; that we should go unto the heathen, and they unto the circumcision.
Galatians 2:9 KJV

To sit at the right hand of an earthly king was a place of honor, denoting special trust, and authority from the king. Those who came to you would give and treat you with respect and obedience, as if you where the king. This was something which was understood without needing an explanation. Jesus is now seated at the "right hand" of the Father according to Mark 16.

After the LORD Jesus had spoken to them, he was taken up into heaven and he sat at the right hand of God.
Then the disciples went out and preached everywhere, and the LORD worked with them and confirmed his words by the signs that accompanied them.
Mark 16:19-20 NIV

No wonder, we have our leaders place their left hand on the Bible and hold up their "right hand" to swear them into office. Satan, as the great counterfeiter, places the mark of the beast in either the forehead or the "right hand," which is the last time the phrase is used in the Bible, Revelation 13:16.

**He required everyone
—small and great, rich and poor, free and slave
—to be given a mark on the right hand or on the forehead.**
Revelation 13:16 NLT

CHAPTER 9

Alms

Alms, and also called almsgiving is a ceremonial, religious act. It involves giving materially, whether it's gold, silver or other items of value to the needy, as a religious virtue. According to the Bible, alms simply mean giving to the poor or needy. This is why the lame man is laid daily at the temple gate called Beautiful, Acts 3. He would ask alms of those who entered the temple at the hour of prayer. Almsgiving was regarded not merely as a righteous act, but also as an act of justice.

The English word "alms" come from the Greek word "eleemosune." It is compare to our modern day word "charity." The word "alms" is actually mentioned 14 times in the King James Bible. It is only written in the books of Matthew, Luke, and Acts of the New Testament. However, the Hebrew word "tsedhaqah" means "righteousness" is the translation for the word "alms," in the Old Testament. Righteousness is the word the Jews used as meanings alms, one example, in the Old Testament is recorded in Daniel 4. In this passage of scriptures, Daniel is speaking to King

Nebuchadnezzar concerning how to lengthen his tranquillity, his peace.

Wherefore, O king (Nebuchadnezzar),
let my (Daniel) **counsel be acceptable unto thee,**
and break off thy sins by <u>righteousness</u>, and
thine iniquities by shewing mercy to the poor;
if it may be a lengthening of thy tranquillity.
Daniel 4:27 KJV

Jesus' first teaching concerning alms is recorded in Matthew 6:1-3.

Take heed that ye do not your alms before men,
to be seen of them:
otherwise ye have no reward of your Father
which is in heaven.
Matthew 6:1 KJV

In Biblical days, there were in every city assigned collectors who distributed alms of two kinds. The first is "the alms of the chest" which is money collected in the synagogue chest every Sabbath for the poor of the city. The second kind of alms was of food and money received in a dish called "alms of the dish." The Pharisees gave much alms, to help the poor and the needy; but only to impress others. The duty was recognized among Christians as extremely important according to, Luke 14:13; Romans 15:25-27; Galatians 2:10.

Only they would that we should remember the poor;

the same which I (Paul) **also was forward to do.**
Galatians 2:10 KJV

A laying of alms in proportion to ones'
resources on every LORD's day is recommended,
1 Corinthians 16:1-4. It also stated that it is a
blessing to give to others, according to Acts 20.

And I (Paul) **have been a constant example
of how you can help those in need by working
hard.
You remember the words of the LORD Jesus,
"It is more blessed to give than to receive."**
Acts 20:35 NLT

Jesus and the twelve disciples set the pattern
for helping the poor in John 13.

**Since Judas was their treasurer,
some thought Jesus was telling him to go
and pay for food or to give some money to the
poor.**
John 13:29 NLT

Each freely gave, and distribution was made,
not to the lazy who would not work, but to the
needy according to Acts 2:45, and 2 Thessalonians
3:10.

**For even when we were with you, this
command you,
that if any would not work, neither should he eat.**

2 Thessalonians 3:10 KJV

It was left to each one's faith and love to give, 2 Corinthians 9:5-8. Remember, God loves a cheerful giver!

Every man according as he purposeth in his heart,
so let him give; not grudgingly, or of necessity: for God loveth a cheerful giver.
2 Corinthians 9:7 KJV

Men of "honest report" were appointed for the distribution of alms, primarily deacons, Acts 6:1-6. Alms are "righteousness," but it doesn't justify a man, Romans, chapters 3, 4, and 5 makes that very clear. Please, Please, Please take time to read these chapters in the name of Jesus Christ, several times.

Almsgiving is doing that which is right for our neighbors, in the court of God's equity, though not in man-made laws. God gives us means for this very end, Ephesians 4:28.

If you are a thief, quit stealing.
Instead, use your hands for good hard work, and give generously to others in need.
Ephesians 4:28 NLT

Almsgiving still exists in a number of religions and regions.

AUTHOR'S CLOSING REMARKS

Peter and John went to church habitually at the 9th hour. They were walking together in unity for the right reason which was for the hour of prayer. They were compassionate toward the needy, sick, lame, and cripple; especially those who lay at the gate begging for alms.

May I say, since Adam and Eve's disobedience, every man and woman is born crippled, it maybe physical, mental or spiritual. God had warned that disobedience to His command would result in death, Genesis 2:16-17. If you remember, Adam didn't instantly fall dead? Oh No, he lived to the age of 930 years! And yet, he did die the exact moment he ate the forbidden fruit.

Since man is a spirit-being, it was into man's spirit that death entered. This does not mean that his spirit ceased to exist, for spiritual death is not a state of non-existence, but rather a state of separation and alienation from God. Spiritual death is separation from God due to sin. Every human being is born crippled with this condition, and only salvation can cure it! When Adam experienced spiritual death in his spirit, his soul and his body also became subjected to the enemy. Romans 5:19 reads, *"For as by one man's disobedience many were made sinners, so by the obedience of one shall many be made righteous."*

Let me say this before I go any farther, man was created by God as a threefold being in the garden of Eden, Genesis 1. We have a spirit known as our inner man; the part of man that knows God, and will live forever in either heaven or hell. Our spirit, inner man is what accepts Jesus Christ as our Lord and Savior.

We have a soul known as the mind. It deals with our intellect, our emotions, and our will. The "intellect" is responsible for our thoughts and reasoning process. The "emotions" controls our temperaments, feelings, attitudes and moods. While the "will" deals with our choices, decisions, and determination.

Then we have the body which is our outward man, the visible house in which man's invisible spirit and soul reside. This part of man provides an external witness to our internal salvation. When Peter healed the lame man, he received strength in his feet and ankle bones. He started walking, leaping, and jumping and praising God. This is considered an outward witness to his inner spiritual salvation.

He was delivered and set free on that day. *Praise the Lord, Saints!*

In a spiritually dead person, the spirit is alienated from God because of sin. Unless he makes a decision to turn from his wick ways, this is a permanent condition! Since the spirit is dead, the soul is now in charge. He is led by his intellect, emotions and will. This person cannot understand spiritual concepts, for they are foreign to him. His body becomes merely a vehicle for acting out his lusts and passions. This man is satan-ruled and death-doomed. In a spiritually alive person, the spirit is back in fellowship with God because of salvation. This is what Peter gave the lame man at gate Beautiful. This truly is a beautiful thing.

I feel like going just a little farther . . .

NOW, there is an ongoing war to subjugate the natural mind and body to God's Spirit now dwelling in the redeemed human spirit, Romans 6:11-14. Romans 7:21-25 is another set of scriptures concerning "The Law and Sin; also Romans 8:1-17, "Living in the Spirit."

Basically, everything that lures, drives, attract, convinces, persuades or motivates us are generated at the intellectual or emotional levels of the mind (soul). Our decisions as to how to react are then made in our mind by our will. The human will is part of the soul that determines our destiny. The soul (mind) is therefore crucial in obtaining salvation, according to Ezekiel 18:20. It reads, ***"The soul that sinneth, it shall die."*** In the process of receiving salvation, our soul repents, our body are baptized, and our spirit is filled with the Holy Ghost.

As a Christian, I no longer have to be controlled and manipulated by the evil forces of the world. I have the Holy Spirit of Jesus Christ living inside of me. Our body is now subject to directions from our reborn spirit, through our soul. It will be our mind that determines the quality of our service to God.

I believe it's crucial to let you know that Satan is powerless as far as the spirit of a man is concerned. He cannot force you to be lost, only you can make that decision. Only by God permission, he is allowed to create troubles, but even then God keeps him on a leash, Job 1:12 and Job 2:6.

The LORD said to Satan,
"Very well, then, everything he has is in your power,
but on the man himself do not lay a finger.
Job 1:12 NIV

The LORD said to Satan,
"Very well, then, he is in your hands;
but you must spare his life.
Job 2:6 NIV

Remember, satan has no power over a child of God, other than what we grant him. He has no authority over us, other than what we surrender to him, and he has no way to hurt us, or destroy us, but his goal is to make us destroy ourselves.

Our will in Christ is greater than man's power according to John 10:28, ***"And I give unto them eternal life; and they shall never perish, neither shall any man pluck them out of my hand."*** Our will in Christ is greater than the devil's power according to 1 John 4:4, ***"Ye are of God, little children, and have overcome them: because greater is he that is in you, than he that is in the world."*** Satan is allowed regular access to you through the mind, this is where the battle begins; the flesh against the spirit. Here, the battle for man's eternal SPIRIT is lost or won. 1 Peter 2:11**, *"Dearly beloved, I beseech you as strangers and pilgrims abstain from fleshly lusts, which war against the soul."***

We know by now that alms simply mean "a donation to the poor." This is what the crippled man kept expecting. He probably was saying, "I need some change!" However, this particular year "He received a change" in the name of Jesus Christ of Nazareth!

I pray that this "Unique and Profound" way that this biblical event that occurred over 2,000 years ago, recorded in Acts 3:1-10, will give you new insight about the word of God. I hope that the following verses, hours, words, numbers, and phrases will always relate to you in a unique and godly manner; this day forward:

1. Acts 3:1-10.

2. The Book of Acts.

3. When you met someone named Peter or John.

4. The following hour of time which you might observe on your watch/clock.

   a. 9 am

   b. 12 noon

   c. 3 pm

5. The word beautiful.

6. The words, colors, or silver and gold coins.

7. A deeper understanding about—Jesus—Christ—of Nazareth.

8. When you shake someone right hand, or even looks at or uses your right hand.

9. The word alms (charity).

10. When you see the numbers 23, 119, or 609, 69? (You got to think a little harder for those last two numbers, but I refer them to the same answer).

**And the peace of God,
which passeth all understanding
shall keep your hearts and minds through
Christ Jesus.**
Philippians 4:7 KJV

ON MY HEART . . .

On July 22, 2012, I attended church at the Salvation Army Rehabilitator Center in Bartlett, Tn. Major Rob Vincent delivered the word of God, "The POWER of God's Word." This message is still ringing in my heart, and it stays on my mind. It had been a long time since a message blessed my soul, "so very much." It makes me howl "Hallelujah" every time I think on it. LORD, I thank you!

In brief . . .

P   is God's Penetrating Power, Hebrew 4:12

O   s God's Overcoming Power, Romans 8:37

W   is God's Wonder Working Power, Luke 5:5

E   is God's Everlasting Power, Matthew 25:24

R   is God's Revealing Power, Hebrew 4:12

I hope and pray, it blesses you to, and help you realize what a might God we serve!

Vanessa Buckhalter

As We wrap up our Ministry with You today;

Will You Pray for the Ministry . . ."Now"

May the "LORD of Peace," Himself give you
Peace at all time and in every way. The LORD be
with you all.

Dr. Vanessa

REFERENCES

Chapter 2

1. Jacksonville Theological Seminary:
   Harmony of the Gospel Class Notes, 10/06

2. Wikipedia, the Free Encyclopaedia: http://
   www.en.wikipedia.org/wiki/Acts

Chapter 3

1. The Apostle Peter: http://www.1way2God.
   net/bio-peter.html

2. Wikipedia, the Free Encyclopaedia:
   http://www.en.wikipedia.org/wiki/
   John_the_Evangelist

Chapter 4

1. The Hours of Prayer/ Biblical Times of
   Memorial:

   http://www.arenessministry.org/
   biblicialhoursofprayer.htm

2. The Seven Historical Hours of Prayer:

    http://prayerfoundation.org/dailyoffice/
    the_seven_hours_of_prayer.htm

Chapter 5

1. Wikipedia, the Free Encyclopaedia:

    http://en.wikepedia/org/wiki/Corinthian_bronze

2. Pilgrimage Panorama:

    http://itsGila.com/tipsgates.htm

Chapter 6

1. Gold: http://www.gold-eagle.com/gold_
    digest_04/stotto62404.html

Chapter 7

1. Jesus Christ—Lord and Savior of the World:
    http://christianity.about.com

2. Wikipedia, the Free Encyclopaedia:

    http://en.wikipedia.org/wiki/Jesus

Chapter 8

1. Right Hand: http://wiki.answers.com/Q/
   What_does_the_right_hand_signigy_in_
   the_Bible

Chapter 9

1. Wikipedia, the Free Encyclopaedia:

   http://en.wikipedia.org/wiki/alms

2. Bible History: http://www.bible-history.com/
   isbe/alms

Answers:

1. Simon, called Peter

2. Andrew his brother

3. James the son of Zebedee

4. John, the brother of James the son of
   Zebedee

5. Philip

6. Bartholomew

7. Thomas

8. Matthew the tax collector

9. James the son of Alphaeus

10. Thaddaeus

11. Simon the Zealot

12. Judas Iscariot, who betrayed Jesus

Answers:

Andrew, Bartholomew, Philip, Simon and Peter were crucified, but Bartholomew was beaten first and Peter was crucified upside down.

James, the son of Alphaeus, Judas (not Iscariot), and Matthias was stoned to death, but Matthias was stoned to death then beheaded.

James, the son of Zebedee, the elder brother of John, and a relative of Jesus, his mother was Salome, the cousin to the Virgin Mary was beheaded.

Matthew and Thomas were speared to death.

John was exiled to the Island of Patmos and later died of old age.

Judas Iscariot hanged himself.

Answer: Matthew 6:9, where the "The LORD Prayer" starts

The Three Daily Historic Prayers:

Psalm 117

[1] Praise the Lord, all you nations; extol him, all you peoples. [2] For great is his love toward us, and the faithfulness of the Lord endures forever. Praise the Lord.

Psalm 23 A psalm of David.

[1] The Lord is my shepherd, I lack nothing. [2] He makes me lie down in green pastures, he leads me beside quiet waters, [3] he refreshes my soul. He guides me along the right paths for his name's sake. [4] Even though I walk through the darkest valley, I will fear no evil, for you are with me; your rod and your staff, they comfort me. [5] You prepare a table before me in the presence of my enemies.

You anoint my head with oil; my cup overflows. [6] Surely your goodness and love will follow me all the days of my life, and I will dwell in the house of the Lord forever.

Matthew 6:9-13

[9] After this manner therefore pray ye: Our Father which art in heaven, Hallowed be thy name. [10] Thy kingdom come, Thy will be done in earth, as it is in heaven. [11] Give us this day our daily bread. [12] And forgive us our debts, as we forgive our debtors. [13] And lead us not into temptation, but deliver us from

evil: For thine is the kingdom, and the power, and the glory, for ever. Amen.

OTHER BOOKS BY THE AUTHOR:

From the Pew to the Pulpit

Isaiah 26:3-4 "Perfect Peace"

Isaiah 26:3-4 "Perfect Peace" The Last Single Digit